LOWDOWN ON
Earthworms

by NORMA DIXON

Fitzhenry & Whiteside

Thanks very much to
Cathy Nesbitt for answering
so many questions and for
a fascinating tour of her
vermicomposting system.

Published in Canada by
Fitzhenry & Whiteside Limited
195 Allstate Parkway
Markham, Ontario   L3R 4T8
www.fitzhenry.ca

Published in the United States by
Fitzhenry & Whiteside,
311 Washington Street,
Brighton, Massachusetts 02135
godwit@fitzhenry.ca

10 9 8 7 6 5 4 3 2 1

National Library of Canada Cataloguing in Publication

Dixon, Norma
     The lowdown on earthworms / Norma Dixon.

ISBN 1-55005-114-8 (bound).—ISBN 1-55005-119-9 (pbk.)

     1. Earthworms—Juvenile literature. I. Title.

QL391.A6D59 2004   j592'.64   C2004-901063-8

Publisher Cataloging-in-Publication Data
(Library of Congress Standards)

Dixon, Norma.
   The lowdown on earthworms / Norma Dixon. _ 1st ed.
[32] p. : ill., photos. (some col.) ;   cm.
ISBN 1-55005-114-8
ISBN 1-55005-119-9 (pbk.)
1. Earthworms — Juvenile literature. (1. Earthworms.)   I. Title.
592.64 dc21   SF597.E3.D59 2004

Fitzhenry & Whiteside acknowledges with thanks the Canada Council for
the Arts, and the Ontario Arts Council for their support of our publishing
program. We acknowledge the financial support of the Government of
Canada through the Book Publishing Industry Development Program
(BPIDP) for our publishing activities.

Canada Council   Conseil des Arts
for the Arts   du Canada

Design by John Luckhurst
Illustrations by Warren Clark

Printed in Singapore

CONTENTS

CHAPTER 1

HUMBLE HEROES

Earthworms are not pretty. They are slimy and squirmy and brown. They have no eyes, ears or legs. Pick one up, and it's as limp as a string. And who can tell its head from its tail?

Don't be fooled by looks. Even without eyes and ears, earthworms can sense when the sun is shining and a hungry mole is nearby. They have no backbone, but they can push stones around and dig deep tunnels. They have a tiny mouth and no teeth, but they spend their lives eating through soil.

Earthworms are equipped for hard work. They are nature's expert recyclers and underground farmers. They plow through the ground eating dead plants and animals and turn all this organic garbage into rich soil. This rich soil grows the plants that all creatures living on the earth need to survive.

Earthworms are nature's humble heroes. They build soil — one of the most important jobs on the planet.

Darwin's Heroes

One person who wasn't fooled by the earthworm's looks was Charles Darwin (1809-1882). This famous English naturalist studied earthworms for almost 40 years. He dug them up on field trips. He kept them in pots in his study. He counted them, blew whistles at them, fed them horseradish and cabbage, and observed them working in his garden.

In 1881, Darwin wrote: "It may be doubted whether there are many other animals which have played so important a part in the history of the world."

No Earthworms, No Pyramids

Today, some scientists say that ancient civilizations might not have developed at all without earthworms. It was the work of worms that improved the river valley soils of Egypt, Mesopotamia and India. This allowed people to start growing agricultural crops about 5,000 years ago. These crops fed the citizens of the world's first villages and towns.

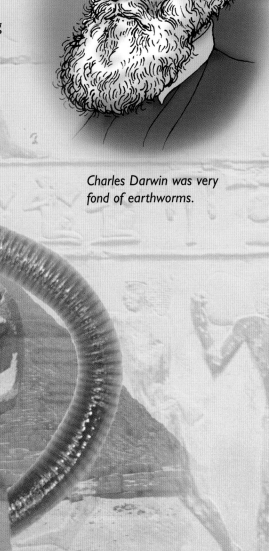

Charles Darwin was very fond of earthworms.

Take a Field Trip

Darwin spent a lot of time outside on his hands and knees searching for earthworms. First, he looked for earthworm evidence. Take a field trip and follow Darwin's clues.

Clues on Top

Darwin carried a cane on his field trips. He poked under piles of leaves looking for signs of burrows and worm casts. You can use a long stick.

Burrows
Earthworms pull leaves into their burrows and then dine underground.

Worm casts
Some worms deposit small piles of waste, called casts, at the top of their burrows.

Digging Down

When you find some worm clues, do what Darwin did. Dig down to see the soil the worms built.

Earthworms make topsoil, a dark layer of earth full of organic matter and plant nutrients.

CHAPTER 2

EARTHWORM I.D.

Many different kinds of wormy creatures live on the planet, but they aren't all earthworms. So how do you know when you're looking at one?

Ring Around the Worms

An earthworm has rings that divide its body into segments. Each segment — except the first and last — has four pairs of tiny bristles. They help the earthworm grip the ground and hold on to the sides of its burrow.

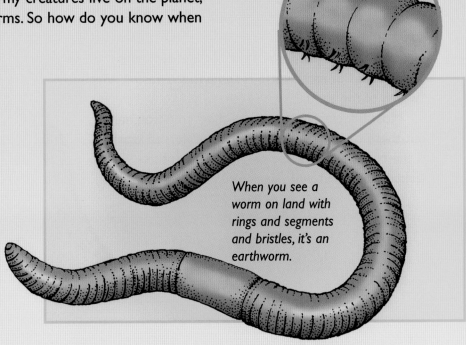

When you see a worm on land with rings and segments and bristles, it's an earthworm.

An Earthworm? Not!

Who are these imposters with worm-like bodies?

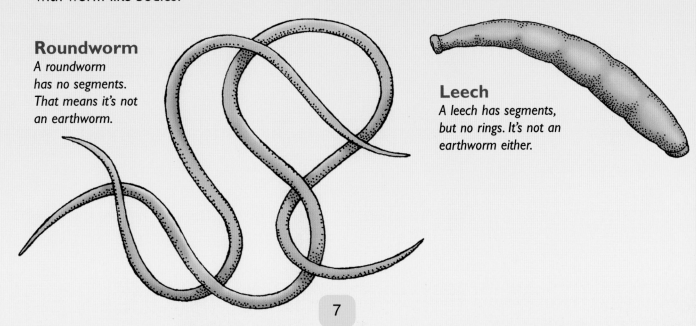

Roundworm
A roundworm has no segments. That means it's not an earthworm.

Leech
A leech has segments, but no rings. It's not an earthworm either.

The Worm Family

Scientists sort animals into families that share characteristics and give them names based on Latin and Greek words. Earthworms belong to the *Annelida Oligochaeta* family, which means "animals with ringed bodies and few bristles."

Inside this big family are smaller families, called species. One species of earthworm is *Lumbricus terrestris*, which means "worm of the earth."

Most people call animals by their common names, but these can be confusing. For example, red worm is the common name for two different species — *Lumbricus rubellus* and *Eisenia fetida*.

Scientific name: *Annelida Oligochaeta Lumbricus rubellus*
Common names: Red worm, red marsh worm

Giants from Down Under

Earthworms come in all sizes. The biggest ones live in warm climates. Australia is home to the Giant Gippsland earthworm. This monster averages 80 cm (32 in.) in length and has 300-500 segments. Its burrows are about 2.5 cm (1 in.) in diameter. Its eggs are the size of small sausages.

Giant Gippsland earthworms spend all their lives underground. That may explain why they were discovered only 100 years ago.

Common Earthworms

The earthworms you're likely to find on field trips are red wigglers, nightcrawlers and red marsh worms. The best way to identify them is by their color, size and habitat.

Worm Studies

Carry a ruler and magnifying glass on field trips. Measure the worms you find. Have a close-up look at their bristles. Count segments.

Red Wiggler

Color: red/brown; some striped
Diameter: like thin string
Length: 4-13 cm (2-5 in.)
Habitat: near surface; under leaves; in manure piles
Scientific name: *Eisenia fetida*
Other common names: red worm, compost worm, manure worm, stink worm

Red Marsh Worm

Color: purple/reddish brown
Diameter: like fat yarn
Length: 6-15 cm (2.5-6 in.)
Habitat: 15-30 cm (6-12 in.) below surface; in orchards
Scientific name: *Lumbricus rubellus*
Other common names: red worm, red wriggler

Nightcrawler

Color: pink/dark reddish brown
Diameter: like a small pencil
Length: 9-30 cm (4-12 in.)
Habitat: in deep burrows, up to 2 m (6 ft) underground
Scientific name: *Lumbricus terrestris*
Other common names: dew worm, garden worm, fish worm

Handle With Care!

It's okay to handle worms if you follow these tips.

- Keep them out of the sun.
- Be gentle.
- Put them back after 10 minutes.
- Wash your hands.

CHAPTER 3

MAKE A WORMERY

A see-through wormery is perfect for worm watching.

You'll need:
- clean plastic water bottle or small aquarium
- utility knife
- hammer and small nail
- garden soil and sand
- spray bottle filled with water
- 3 to 10 earthworms
- tape

How to make it:
1. If you're making a water-bottle wormery, ask an adult to help you use the utility knife to cut off the top of the bottle. With the hammer and nail, make small air holes in the bottom and in the cap.
2. Fill the bottom half of the wormery with garden soil. Cover with a layer of sand, about 5 cm (2 in.). Fill to the top with garden soil.
3. Spray water on the soil. It should be damp but not wet.
4. Place the worms on top of the soil. Add small bits of vegetable leaves.
5. For the water-bottle wormery, tape the top on the bottom and add the cap. For the aquarium, place a cover with air holes on top.
6. Place the wormery in a cool spot out of direct sunlight.
7. Once a week, feed the worms more leaves.

Please, Release Me!

Worms will stay healthy in a wormery for a few weeks. Then it's time to release them back into the wild. Empty the wormery on the soil in a garden or park. Cover the worms with leaves to protect them from predators and sunlight.

Worm Watching

Earthworms are nocturnal animals, which means they are most active at night. You'll have to trick them if you want to watch them during the day. Try covering the wormery with a black cloth for a few hours.

Earthworms make burrows by eating through the soil.

The layer of sand gets mixed into the garden soil as the worms travel through their burrows.

Worms come to the surface to find food and then drag it into their burrows.

CHAPTER 4

OUTSIDE BODY PARTS

The earthworm has no big body parts, like arms and legs, sticking out.
That gives it a streamlined tube shape — perfect for moving around underground.

Mouth: At the front of the first segment is a tiny, toothless mouth.

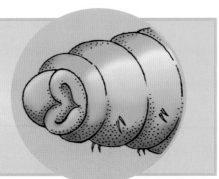

Prostomium: Under the mouth is a sensitive lip called a prostomium. It helps the worm find food and pull it into its burrow.

Skin: The skin has cells that are sensitive to light, touch and vibrations. It produces a slimy mucus that helps the worm breathe.

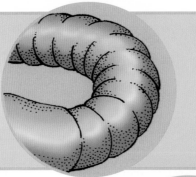

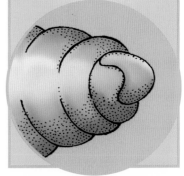

Anus: At the end of the last segment is the anus, an opening for getting rid of wastes after the worm has digested its food.

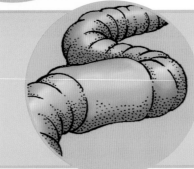

Saddle: A swollen segment near the head end is called a saddle, or clitellum. Worms mate by joining at the clitellum.

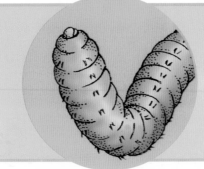

Bristles: Tiny bristles, called setae, grip the ground and anchor the worm inside its burrow when predators try to yank it out.

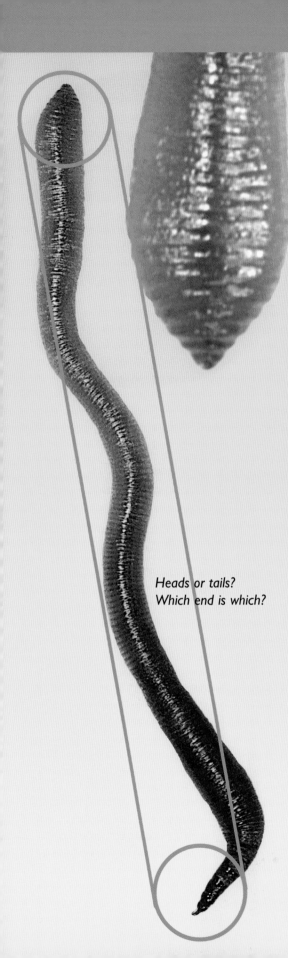

Heads or tails?
Which end is which?

Heads or Tails?

One way to tell which end is which is by watching an earthworm move. It's usually travelling head first. Or look for the worm's mouth and prostomium with a magnifying glass.

No Heads, No Tails

Can an earthworm that's been cut in half grow a new head or tail? Depending on where the worm is cut, the part with the head might grow a new tail. But most biologists believe that the cut-off tail cannot grow a new head.

In the Skin of a Worm

The worm's skin produces slimy stuff called mucus. It keeps the worm slippery so it can slither through tight tunnels. It also keeps the worm breathing. Oxygen in the air dissolves in the mucus, passes through the skin and into the bloodstream, and then gets carried to all the worm's body parts.

Sensitive Cells

An earthworm has cells in its skin that are sensitive to light, vibrations and touch. Light-sensitive cells protect it from the sun. If it's stuck in the sun, its slimy skin dries out, no oxygen gets through, and the worm suffocates. Vibration-sensitive cells warn that predators are nearby. The worm senses their vibrations through the ground — just in time for a quick getaway.

Darwin's Experiments

Darwin kept pots of worms in his study so he could observe their behavior and conduct simple experiments. Try his experiments to find out how your worms behave.

Candlelight

At night, Darwin shone a candle on his worms. "When a worm is suddenly illuminated," he observed, "it dashes like a rabbit into its burrow." Use a flashlight for your experiment. What happens if you cover the flashlight with a piece of red cellophane?

Their sensitivity to light protects worms from drying out in the sun.

Musical Vibrations

When Darwin shouted or whistled at his worms, they "remained perfectly quiet." But when he placed a pot of worms on top of a piano and banged loud notes, they disappeared into their burrows in a flash.

How do your worms behave when you march around them beating a drum? Observe what happens when you set your drum on the wormery and beat it again.

Darwin concluded that worms can't detect sound waves in the air, but are very sensitive to vibrations travelling through solid objects.

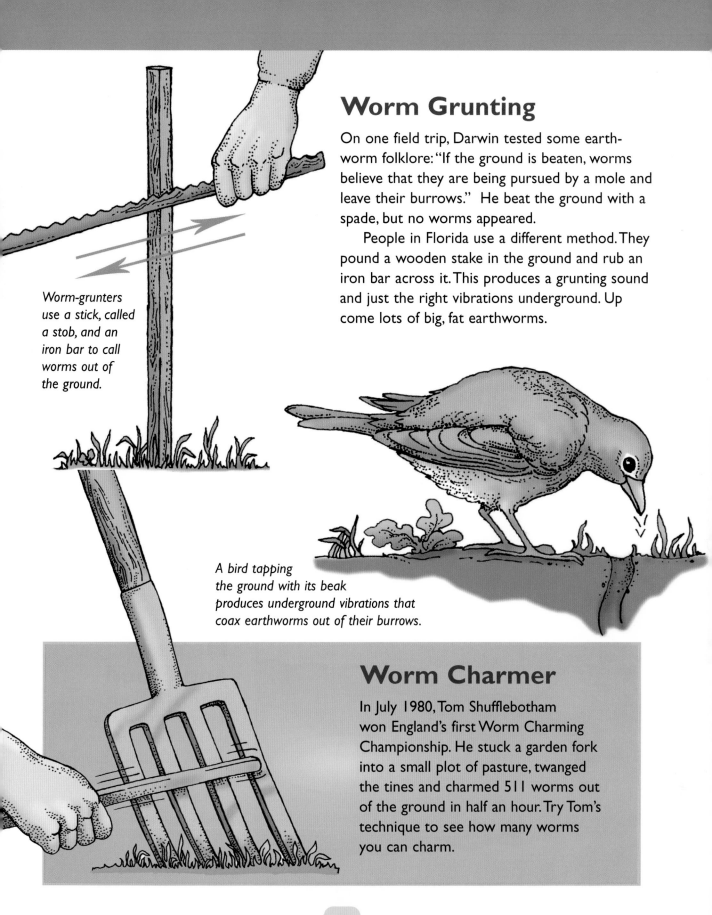

Worm Grunting

On one field trip, Darwin tested some earthworm folklore: "If the ground is beaten, worms believe that they are being pursued by a mole and leave their burrows." He beat the ground with a spade, but no worms appeared.

People in Florida use a different method. They pound a wooden stake in the ground and rub an iron bar across it. This produces a grunting sound and just the right vibrations underground. Up come lots of big, fat earthworms.

Worm-grunters use a stick, called a stob, and an iron bar to call worms out of the ground.

A bird tapping the ground with its beak produces underground vibrations that coax earthworms out of their burrows.

Worm Charmer

In July 1980, Tom Shufflebotham won England's first Worm Charming Championship. He stuck a garden fork into a small plot of pasture, twanged the tines and charmed 511 worms out of the ground in half an hour. Try Tom's technique to see how many worms you can charm.

CHAPTER 5

INSIDE BODY PARTS

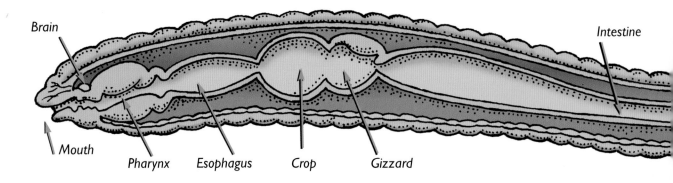

Brain

Intestine

Mouth

Pharynx   Esophagus   Crop   Gizzard

Brain and Nerves

The worm's tiny brain is in its first segment. Connected to it are two threads of a nerve chord that run along the top and bottom of the worm's body. Three pairs of nerves branch off into each segment. The nerves receive messages from sensitive cells located in the worm's skin.

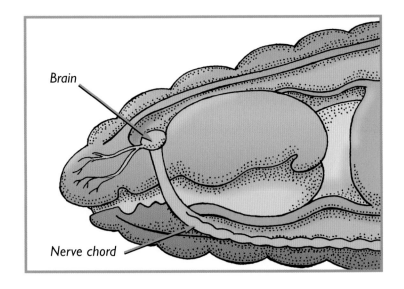

Brain

Nerve chord

Five pairs of hearts

Blood vessels

Hearts and Blood

Five pairs of hearts pump a worm's blood. It flows through three main blood vessels and then into smaller ones. They carry oxygen and food nutrients to every segment.

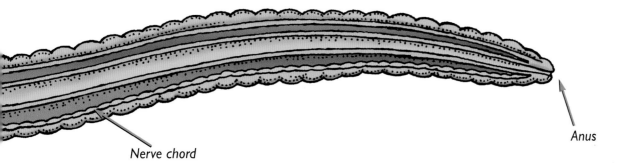

Nerve chord

Anus

Diet and Digestion

Earthworms eat soil, decaying plants and seeds, insect eggs and larva, and body parts of dead bugs and small animals. This organic diet moves through the worm's very efficient digestive system.

Pharynx: Muscles in the pharynx pull food through the worm's mouth and push it into the esophagus.

Esophagus and Crop: The esophagus passes food into the crop, where it sits in storage.

Gizzard: Food travels into the gizzard. Particles of sand and grit — leftovers in the worm's soil diet — grind the food into tiny bits.

Intestine: Food bits move into the long intestine. Nutrients pass through the intestine walls, into the bloodstream, and then into the worm's cells.

Anus: Leftover wastes move through the intestine and out the anus, a small opening on the last segment.

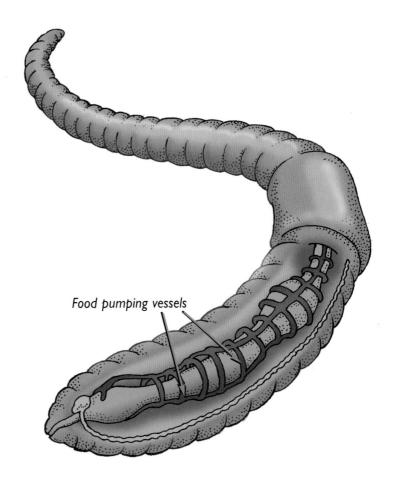

Food pumping vessels

Eating Habits

Charles Darwin discovered that worms liked some foods better than others. His were very fond of horseradish. In one experiment, Darwin sprinkled red and green cabbage on the top of his pots of worms. The worms devoured the green cabbage first. In another, he offered bits of leaves from cabbage, turnip, beet and celery, along with a few carrot tops. Carrot tops won.

Food Experiment

Try Darwin's menu in your wormery.

1. Choose two or three different kinds of vegetable leaves. Break them into small bits.

2. Place each food choice in a different spot on the soil. Make a toothpick flag so you'll remember where things are.

3. Check the wormery to see which food the worms pull into their burrows first.

Beet Leaves

Celery Leaves

Carrot Leaves

Moving Right Along

A moving worm makes slow but steady progress. Using its bristles and two sets of muscles, a worm stretches out, scrunches up and inches forward. With each effort, it moves 2-3 cm (1-1.5 in.).

1 *First, the worm grips the soil with its rear-end bristles.*

2 *Then, it squeezes the short, circular muscles that form rings around its body. This makes the worm's body stretch out and move forward.*

3 *Next, the rear-end bristles let go and the worm anchors itself with its front-end bristles.*

4 *Finally, the worm squeezes the long muscles that run from its head to its tail. This makes the worm's body scrunch up and its back end move forward.*

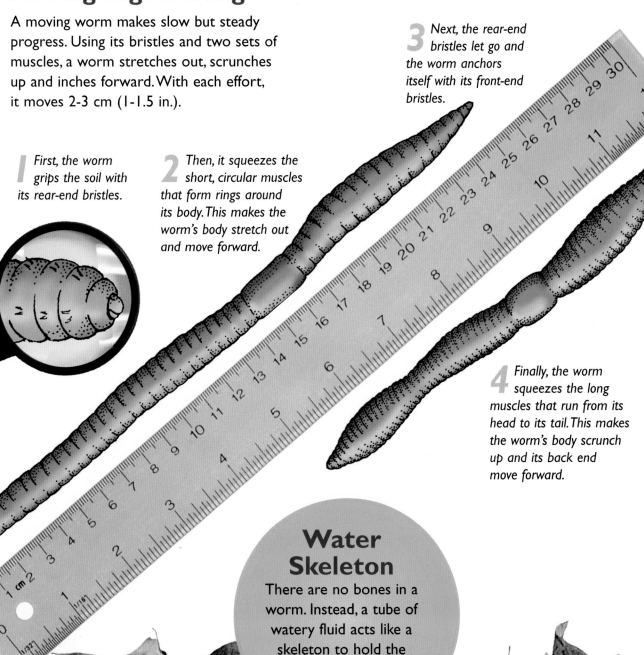

Water Skeleton

There are no bones in a worm. Instead, a tube of watery fluid acts like a skeleton to hold the worm's body in shape.

CHAPTER 6

LIFE IN THE BURROWS

Some earthworm species live in deep burrows, and others stay closer to the top of the ground. How deep an earthworm dwells depends on its eating habits.

Home Is Where the Food Is

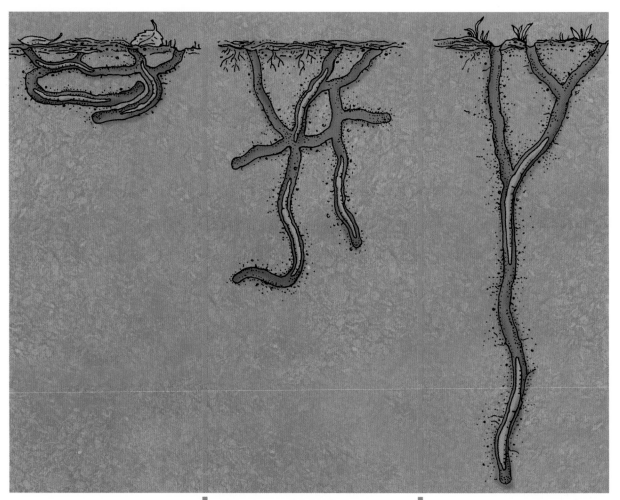

Litter Dwellers
Red wigglers (*Eisenia fetida*) eat organic matter that collects on top of the soil, especially decomposing leaves and manure. They live in untidy burrows just below the surface.

Shallow Dwellers
Red marsh worms (*Lumbricus rubellus*) eat topsoil that's full of plant roots and other organic matter. Their burrows are 15-30 cm (6-12 in.) deep and branch out through the topsoil.

Deep Dwellers
Nightcrawlers (*Lumbricus terrestris*) dig their burrows straight down, about 1-2 m (3-6 ft) deep. They come to the surface to collect food and then pull it into their burrows.

Burrow Facts

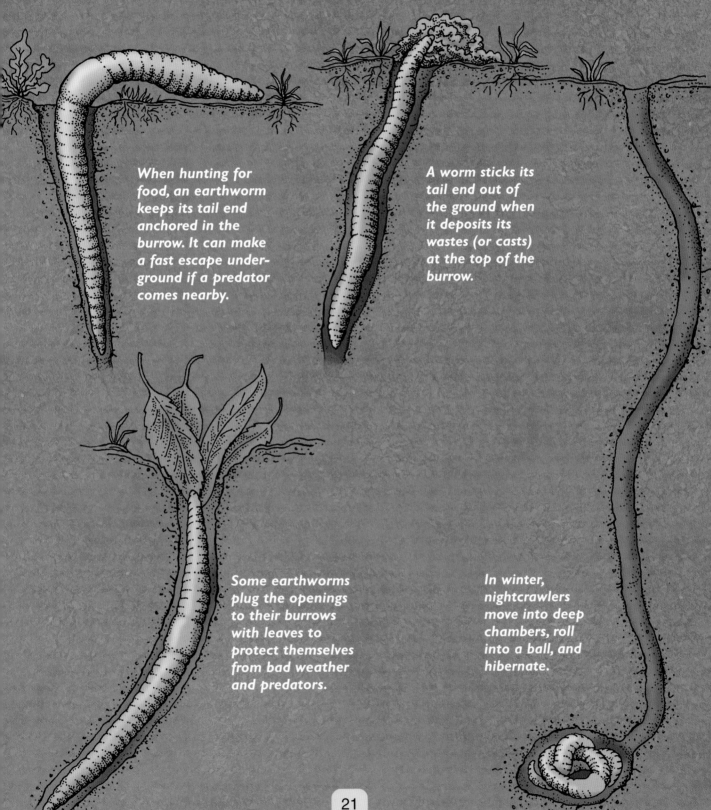

When hunting for food, an earthworm keeps its tail end anchored in the burrow. It can make a fast escape underground if a predator comes nearby.

A worm sticks its tail end out of the ground when it deposits its wastes (or casts) at the top of the burrow.

Some earthworms plug the openings to their burrows with leaves to protect themselves from bad weather and predators.

In winter, nightcrawlers move into deep chambers, roll into a ball, and hibernate.

Life Cycle

The life of a wild worm is dangerous. That may be one reason why it has a special reproductive system. Each worm produces its own sperm and eggs.

When two worms mate, each one creates a new generation of worms. Animals that have both male and female reproductive organs, like earthworms, are called hermaphrodites.

Mating Worms

Mating worms lie head to tail, joined at the clitellum. Each worm collects sperm from its partner, then returns to its burrow.

Eggs and Cocoon

Underground, fertilized eggs develop inside a cocoon. It swells and darkens close to hatching time.

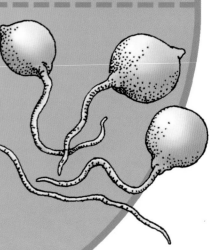

Adult

When its clitellum has developed, the worm looks for a mate. And the cycle begins again.

Hatchling

A just-hatched worm is as thin as a thread and almost colorless. But it's ready to eat and burrow.

Life Span

All species of earthworms go through the same stages of the life cycle, but some live longer and others produce more eggs. It all depends on where they live.

Red wigglers live close to the surface of the ground. Most individuals are killed by predators or dry weather a year or two after they hatch. But the species (*Eisenia fetida*) survives because each worm produces up to 900 eggs a year.

Nightcrawlers (*Lumbricus terrestris*) hide from predators and bad weather in deep underground burrows. This species lives as long as six years, and produces about 40 cocoons a year.

Enemies Above and Below

Above ground, foxes, badgers, frogs, toads, turtles, snakes and birds hunt for earthworms because they are a rich source of protein.

Down below, the worm's worst enemy is the mole.

CHAPTER 7

A WORM'S WORLD

An earthworm's world is a busy place. It's a community full of plants and animals that depend on each other and their environment for everything they need — air, water, soil, food and shelter. This kind of community is called an ecosystem.

An earthworm hides in its burrow chewing on a dry leaf. A nightcrawler is eating through the soil as it heads deeper underground. Down below, its cocoons are starting to hatch. A mole lurks nearby.

A field mouse nibbles the fresh shoots of a wildflower. Its young wait for food in their nest underground. A bird taps the ground with its beak trying to coax an earthworm out of its burrow.

Plants thrive in the earthworm's world. In spring, seeds germinate in the fine topsoil earthworms make. Young plants send roots down burrows that fill up with the air and moisture they need to grow. They feed on the nutrients and minerals that worms deposit and mix through the soil. When plants die, earthworms recycle their organic waste and turn it back into rich soil for the next generation.

Earthworms at Work

Here are some amazing facts about how hard earthworms work.

* In one day, an earthworm can eat organic matter that weighs as much as it does. Can you imagine eating your body weight in food everyday?

* Charles Darwin collected and weighed worm casts to find out how much of their fertile manure earthworms deposited on an acre (4,000 m²) each year. In a meadow near his home, it amounted to a whopping 18 tons (18,000 kg).

* Earthworms have been building topsoil for millions of years. One scientist says that, if all this topsoil was piled in one spot, it would make a mountain five times higher than Mount Everest.

* Earthworms spend their lives breaking down organic matter. In a world without worms, we'd all be buried under mountains of dry leaves and dead bugs.

CHAPTER 8

MAKE A WORM COMPOSTING BIN

Make a habitat-in-a-bin for earthworms and watch them recycle organic leftovers from your kitchen into rich compost — the perfect food for plants.

The Worms

This worm bin makes a good home for red wigglers (*Eisenia fetida*). It's similar to their habitat in the wild where they live just below the ground and eat lots of organic matter in the topsoil. You can also use red marsh worms (*Lumbricus rubellus*). But no nightcrawlers, please! This species (*Lumbricus terrestris*) lives deep underground and won't survive in the shallow soil of a worm bin.

You'll need lots of worms — about 300-500. It's best to buy them from a vermicomposter. That's a worm expert who raises and sells composting worms.

You'll need:
250 g (1/2 pound) of red wigglers or red marsh worms

Buy your worms from worm farmers or vermicomposters. They are full of expert advice for setting up and maintaining a worm bin.

The Bin

You can make a worm bin from a wood or plastic container. Before making the bin, figure out where you'll be keeping it. An ideal spot is in a dark area, out of the sun, with a temperature of 20-25 C (68-78 F). Some people set their bins under the kitchen sink.

You'll need:

- old wooden drawer or box or plastic bin, about 30-45 cm (12-18 in.) deep
- screen for bottom
- bin cover
- air holes
- large tray
- bricks or wood blocks

How to make it:

1. Ask an adult to help you make holes for air and drainage in the bottom and near the top of each side of the bin. The holes should be 6 mm (1/4 in.) in diameter and about 10-15 cm (4-6 in.) apart.
2. Place the screen in the bottom of the bin.
3. Put the tray under the bin to catch any drips that leak through.
4. Set the bin on bricks or wood blocks so air can circulate under it.

The Bedding

Your worms need bedding they can live in and eat. The best bedding is newspaper cut into small strips with a mixture of grass clippings or dry leaves.

1. Add bedding until the bin is about three-quarters full. Spray it with water until it's damp, but not soggy wet.
2. Mix in a few handfuls of garden soil and two or three crushed egg shells.
3. Fluff up the bedding so it's loose and full of air pockets.
4. Put the worms on top and add the cover. Let them adjust to their new habitat for a day before adding food.

Feeding the Worms

Every few days, bury your kitchen leftovers in a different spot, just under the surface. Sprinkle a handful of bedding on top. Once a week, add a few crushed egg shells.

Good Food
fruits, vegetables
coffee grounds, tea bags
egg shells, bread, oatmeal
dried leaves, composted manure

Bad Food
dairy products
meat and bones
pet poop

Harvesting Compost

In a few months, the worms will turn their food and bedding into compost. Dump the bin onto a big plastic sheet, and remove the worms by hand. Watch for worm cocoons and tiny hatchlings. Place them all back in the bin with fresh bedding and food. Sprinkle the compost around plants in your house and garden.

Glossary

Bristles are tiny, stiff hairs that help the worm move and anchor itself in the soil. They are also called setae.

Burrows are tunnels that worms make as they eat through soil.

Casts (or castings) are worm wastes that are full of plant nutrients.

Clitellum is a swollen segment on the worm's body. It produces mucus that forms the cocoons.

Cocoon holds the fertilized eggs until they are ready to hatch.

Compost is a mixture of decayed organic matter that gardeners use to improve soil.

Composting bin is a plastic or wood container filled with earthworms and organic matter. The worms eat through the organic matter and turn it into compost.

Ecosystem is a community of plants and animals and other living things that share a habitat and are linked together in a food web.

Habitat is the place where a plant or animal makes its home in nature.

Hatchlings are worms that have just hatched from a cocoon.

Hermaphrodite is an animal that has both male and female sex organs.

Humus is the dark brown part of soil that is formed from organic matter.

Naturalist is a person who studies things in nature.

Nocturnal means "at night." Nocturnal animals are active mostly at night.

Organic matter is material from plants and animals.

Prostomium is the earthworm's lip. It has sensitive cells that help the worm find food.

Saddle. *See Clitellum*

Segment is a section of an earthworm's body.

Setae. *See Bristles*

Species is a family of animals that can breed and produce young.

Topsoil is the rich, dark, upper layer of soil that contains humus and plant nutrients.

Vermicomposter is a person who uses worms to turn organic matter into compost.

Bibliography and Further Reading

Appelhof, Mary. *Worms Eat My Garbage: How to Set Up and Maintain a Worm Composting System.* Kalamazoo: Flower Press, 1997.

Buchsbaum, Ralph, Mildred Buchsbaum, John Pearse and Vicki Pearse. *Animals Without Backbones.* Chicago: University of Chicago Press, 1987.

Darling, Lois, and Louis Darling. *Worms.* New York: William Morrow, 1972.

Darwin, Charles. *The Formation of Vegetable Mould Through the Action of Worms, with Observations on Their Habits.* Reprint, London: Faber & Faber, 1945.

Himmelman, John. *An Earthworm's Life.* New York: Children's Press, 2001.

Levine, Shar. *The Worm Book.* Toronto: Somerville House, 1997.

McFarland, David, ed. *The Oxford Companion to Animal Behavior.* New York: Oxford University Press, 1982.

McLaughlin, Molly. *Earthworms, Dirt and Rotten Leaves.* New York: Avon Books, 1990.

Minnich, Jerry. *The Earthworm Book.* Emmaus, Pennsylvania: Rodale Press, 1977.

Nancarrow, Loren. *The Worm Book: The Complete Guide to Worms in Your Garden.* Berkeley: Ten Speed Press, 1998.

Nesbitt, Cathy. Interview about Vermicomposting. March 2004. Bradford, Ontario.

Pascoe, Elaine. *Earthworms.* Woodbridge, Connecticut: Blackbirch Press, 1997.

Earthworm Web Sites:

BioKids: http://www.biokids.umich.edu/critters/information/Oligochaeta.html

Cathy's Crawly Composters: http://www.cathyscomposters.com

Discovery Kids: http://yucky.kids.discovery.com/flash/worm/pg000102.html

Worm Watch Canada: http://www.naturewatch.ca/english/wormwatch

Worm Woman: http://www.wormwoman.com/acatalog/index.html

Worm World: http://www.zephyrus.co.uk/wormworld.html

Index